Only One Surrender is a beautiful testament to the life and work of Saucha Gavin Harrison. His devotion to the unity of truth and love permeated every aspect of his life and was an inspiration to everyone who knew him. And Rashani Rea's collages give remarkable visual expression to the depth and transformative power of Gavin's wise and loving words.

—**Joseph Goldstein**, author of *Mindfulness: A Practical Guide to Awakening*

Rashani Rea's art shimmers with evocativeness — though what is evoked is not the conditioned mind, it is a grand stirring of the heart. Her work, in combination with Saucha Gavin Harrison's wise pointing, does not provoke thought, it stills it. Experiencing the intermingling of their crafts is like witnessing two whirling dervishes spinning in divine devotion, turning in the same direction, in the name of God. Two devotees in solitude with their love, yet spinning, in unison. In the recognition and direct experience of oneness. This book sings.

—**Caverly Morgan**, founder and guiding teacher of Presence Collective and Peace in Schools

Gavin Saucha Harrison held a unique place in our community and in the Dharma teacher's network as a Dharma mystic whose heart, mind, and body had been busted open to a profound depth of compassion and insight through the unique mix of human sufferings he had intimate encounters with. His transparency, vulnerability, strength, wisdom, and creative spirit expressed a worldview that invited us all to expand our horizons of human nature and human potential. This beautifully crafted creative offering of Gavin's teachings and Rashani's rich imagery is a glowing tribute for us to carry his wisdom and love with us along The Way.

—**Joel & Michelle Levey**, founders: Wisdom at Work; authors, *Living in Balance: A Mindful Guide for Thriving in a Complex World*, and fellow explorers of mystical terrain with Gavin and Rashani for many years…!

This book honoring the much beloved Saucha Gavin Harrison is a gem, gorgeous and transporting. Each page offers an exquisite blend of sacred poetry and imagery that nourishes the soul.

—**Tara Brach**, author of *Radical Acceptance* and *True Refuge: Finding Peace and Freedom in Your Own Awakened Heart*

Rashani's tribute to Saucha Gavin Harrison is an illuminating invitation to Grace. With few words, Saucha Gavin says so very much. A beauty-full book that radiates love and remembrance.

—**Jeff Brown**, author of *Grounded Spirituality* and *An Uncommon Bond*

Only One Surrender is exceptionally beautiful. Rashani's inspiration and creativity are alive on the pages in a way that communicates profound stillness—a masterful achievement!

—**Juju of Ka'u**, poet and writer

When selflessness meets selflessness, then manifests into being something that can be shared with others, lives are transformed and the magnificence of consciousness expands. In this exquisite offering, the depth of awareness that flows from Rashani's art is combined, in humble reverence, with the timeless wisdom of Saucha Gavin Harrison, offering those fortunate enough to absorb these pages a priceless gift.

—**Kathy Douglas**, Filmmaker: *Finding Compás* and *The Song Within Sedona*

Rashani has produced yet another beautiful and heart-felt creation, another book of dedication and collages that are likened to prayers to the Beloved. Saucha Gavin Harrison's life was a life well lived in service to humanity. Rashani captures his essence, his life's purpose and his importance to her in this new book that celebrates his life. *Only One Surrender* is an act of love for Saucha Gavin as well as a gift to the many of us who have also lost our dear friends.

—**Diane Steinbrecher**, nondual psychotherapist, consultant, teacher and co-author of *The Treasure Within: An Archetypal Unfolding to Your Infinite Potential*

The words and poetry of Saucha Gavin Harrison are a beautiful reminder to us all of how to live full lives as the profound, complex, compassionate, and clear-sighted beings we truly are. This selection of Gavin's words, blended with Rashani Réa's exquisite visual meditations in color and texture and form, invite us to surrender into the deeper rhythms of ourselves. I keep returning to the poet's gentle reminder, "Give way into the sacred arc of your life."

—**Ivan M. Granger**, editor of *This Dance of Bliss: Ecstatic Poetry from Around the World*

Words by Saucha Gavin Harrison stop time; still chatter, return focus. The images by Rashani stir the umbilical cord that connects me to "this volcanic paradise of paradox." I am humbled and filled with gratitude for their example and invitation to manifest the divine.

—**Catherine Kalama Becker**, author of *Mana Cards: The Power of Hawaiian Wisdom*

Only Rashani Réa, with her luminous blend of quietude and ecstasy, could possibly convey through images the passionate presence of such a soul as Gavin Harrison's. My life was blessed when he entered it, and there is a hole in the world where he left it. Yet that space is spilling over with light.

–**Mirabai Starr**, author of *Caravan of No Despair* and *Wild Mercy*

Only One Surrender is one of the most beautiful weddings of Art and Wisdom I have encountered. It is a perfect and gentle introduction to the words of a unique teacher, edited with subtle mastery and illustrated brilliantly.

–**William Martin**, author of *The Activist's Tao Te Ching: Ancient Advice for a Modern Revolution*

Rashani's art is visceral. It penetrates beyond cognition straight to the soma and the heart. It expands awareness. It's a free ticket for "what is." In the art of psychology, we somewhat struggle to surrender cognition. The content, the narrative takes too much space. Rashani and Saucha Gavin provide a direct connection with that healing force that empowers our being to become our true self.

–**Smadar de Lange** Ph.D., clinical psychologist

Immersing oneself in the collages and poems in this book warms the heart like the deep embrace of a timeless lover. It is refreshing, in this era of many distractions, to engage in this kind of collaborative art that truly touches the heart of this moment. Through the portal of this book I found a possibility of grace, self-love and forgiveness. It draws us back to the bare essentials.

–**Yoav Melamed**, earth custodian and community organizer, co-founder of Waianaia Earth Temple

In the dance between illustration and word, this book touches the very Heart of both the endless and the sweetly vulnerable—in an invitation to our deepest intimacy with reality. Profoundly touching. Thank you Rashani and Gavin.

–**Aisha Salem**, spiritual guide

Thank you, Rashani Réa, for remembering our dear friend Saucha Gavin Harrison in such a remarkable way. *Only One Surrender* is guaranteed to massage the heart of anyone who ever had the good fortune to know him in this lifetime. And what an introduction for someone who is just now discovering a new friend. The interrelatedness between the subtle beauty of the visual images and the succinct clarity of words will surely be inspiring generations to come.

–**Dhiresha McCarver**, author of *The Photographic I Ching*

Saucha Gavin Harrison embodied wisdom and clarity, a Buddha-full being. Rashani Réa is an artist of the soul, a wise woman, a living conduit of Grace. *Only One Surrender: By Happenstance and Grace* is testament to All That Is Reveling in sacred text; magnified and sanctified by holy image. Reflections of Pure Being. This sacred water is a blessing for all.

–**Steven L. Schatz**, founder of the Center for Music & Imagery/Psychosynthesis; author of several books

The artwork by Rashani in this book, *Only One Surrender: By Happenstance and Grace* goes beyond artwork. It is a mystical journey into the heart of Saucha Gavin's beautiful being. The excerpts of his poems interwoven into Rashani's collages create a beautiful dance into the mystery that Gavin's teachings were all about.

–**Jatta Tapio**, "takes one lunatic to recognize another"

Only One Surrender embraces a most beautiful expression of poetry and art from which everyone nurturing their heart of compassion and joy could benefit. Rashani Réa's artwork offers a perfectly seamless presentation and tribute to the passing of our dear Dharma brother Saucha Gavin Harrison and his delicious poetic expressions of heart-fullness. Being neither a poet nor an artist myself, this book has me feeling rather awed by how deeply inspiring these combined expressions of that one true surrender can be. My faith in the way of awakening that we have shared for so many years leaves no room for doubt that when the moment of truth appeared for Saucha Gavin—the moment that reveals no boundary between the illusions of birth and death—his surrender found completion, and his heart felt nothing but boundless joy in the presence of emptiness.

–**Erik Knud-Hansen**, the Dharma of Nonduality and author of *Imperience: Understanding the Heart of Consciousness*

The artwork in this book is absolutely beautiful. Rashani's collages combined with the mystical writings of our beloved Gavin offer a deep and passionate spiritual wisdom. It shall be treasured by anyone who is open to a deeper knowing of the Heart.

–**Devaji**, spiritual teacher, author of *Illuminated by Love*

Only One Surrender is a beautiful offering from the heart to the heart. Each page is a transmission of love and essential wisdom, inviting us to be intimately with our hearts.

–**Zaya Benazzo**, filmmaker and a co-founder of the SAND conference

ONLY ONE SURRENDER
By Happenstance and Grace

Collages by Rashani Réa
Poetry by Saucha Gavin Harrison

Foreword by Trudy Goodman

SACRED SPIRAL PRESS

P.O. Box 916
Naʻalehu
Hawaiʻi
96772
808 929-8043
www.rashani.com

ONLY ONE SURRENDER: By Happenstance and Grace

First Edition

Epigraph © David Whyte, 2015

"When Death Comes" © Mary Oliver, date unknown

Foreword © Trudy Goodman, 2019

Poetry and words from newsletters © Saucha Gavin Harrison, 2018

Cover design, introduction, and collages © Rashani Réa, 2019

ISBN: 9781796585308

TO THOSE WHOSE LIVES WERE TOUCHED AND TRANSFORMED BY SAUCHA GAVIN HARRISON

The only choice we have as we mature
is how we inhabit our vulnerability,
how we become larger and more courageous
and more compassionate through our
intimacy with disappearance.

–David Whyte

Love serves as my guide to the very end.
All alone, toward the majestic Friend
I walk kissing the ground—and I arrive.

–Yunus Emre

FOREWORD

Only One Surrender is a magnificent paean to the lyrical poetry and mystical art born from Gavin Harrison's passionate union with the Beloved and Rashani Réa's creative gifts. Rashani has created luminous images to accompany selections from Gavin's poems. This is a gorgeous book, a loving panegyric on the ineffable reality we call God, Unconditional Love, True Nature. Both Gavin and Rashani are life-long mystics and activists, inviting us to soar on a magic carpet ride across the Indescribable—pointed to in Gavin's poems and Rashani's art.

35 years ago—in Brattleboro, Vermont, Adelaide Harrison, a sweet white-haired lady from South Africa was visiting her son Gavin, my long-time friend. She confided to me in a hushed voice when he left the room, "He only does what he wants to do!" She was shocked at her son's commitment to listening to his body and his willingness to trust his intuition 100%, even if it meant disappointing people. I tried to reassure her: he's not being selfish, he's following in the footsteps of the Buddha, who taught that the best way to care for others is to be sure we're taking wise care of our own life energy, too.

Gavin was diagnosed with HIV back when it was a death sentence, before the antiretroviral medicines that save lives. For the first year after his diagnosis, he came to live with my wasband (former husband) and me in Cambridge. Thanks to his fierce commitment to sustaining the health of his body and the support of his friends and fans, he was graced with enough additional years to fulfill his spiritual longing. Gavin lived a truly enlightened life of meditation, beauty, service and joy. From his work with children orphaned by the AIDS epidemic in South Africa and with gay men living with HIV in the early days, to his spirited teaching, Gavin used his passion and talents to share the Dharma he loved.

After years of sickness with HIV, Gavin moved from wintry New England to Hawai'i's tropical climate. There, he managed to live well and thrive. If there was something special he felt called to do, Gavin would negotiate with the virus, whom he named "Sipho" ('gift' in Zulu, Xhosa.) For example: "Sipho, how about this? We'll rest now if we can go to the poetry reading later." This is not to say Gavin appreciated the 'gift.' He was pragmatic. The virus was a presence in his life. He had to find a way to peacefully co-exist with it. As he said, "the virus has been the fieriest teacher!"

Once he was settled on the Big Island, Gavin experienced an explosion of creativity. He made colorful pastels of the undersea world he discovered snorkeling along the Waimea coastline. He found a piano and played exquisitely, everything from show tunes to jazz improv to classics. Then came the poetry. The ecstatic Sufi poets, Rumi and Hafiz, gave him a vision of life lived in full-on joyous surrender. He felt them at his back when his own poems began "flowering from the ground of love that was always there, awaiting my arrival!"

I'd never been to Hawai'i before when he invited me to come teach. He drove us all around the entire island. We slept in tents, saw desert landscapes, ancient temples "Heiau," ocean life, and woke to the sound of mourning doves and geckos. I learned about the rich Polynesian island culture, still alive despite over a century of colonialism and appropriation. Gavin fell in love with Hawai'i's land and people, reminiscent of his beloved homeland in South Africa. He dove heart-first into island life and was eager to share what he discovered.

During many visits over the years, we walked ridges and hiked down to sacred valleys tucked between towering misty mountains. We snorkeled way out along the reefs of Waiaiea Bay, Puako, and Mahukona. I slept under the stars on the beach where green turtles swim in between the rocks at nightfall to clamber up on the sand and sleep. We wandered among giant ferns in the rainforest of Volcano, drove along a coastal road long since buried by lava, walked carefully out across a rugged moonscape of sharp black lava rock. We stopped to pay homage to Pele, the goddess of volcanoes, with traditional offerings of flowers and gin.

Awe-struck and reverent, I witnessed the earth giving birth to herself, erupting in rivers of burning liquefied rock—long, slow cascades of flame flowing down the mountainside from the crater of Kilauea, an active volcano on the flank of Mauna Loa. With fascination and wonder, I watched lava creep inexorably towards the road, overtaking little trees and grasses that burst into flame at its touch. We tiptoed quickly over cooled lava that can be molten underneath, suddenly blazing up into fire with no warning. I admired Gavin's wild fearlessness mixed with mindful care. With his mélange of intense enthusiasm and respect, Hawaiian history came alive before my eyes.

During the years of his teaching on the Big Island, Gavin's meditation groups blossomed in Waimea, Kapa'au, and Kona, responding to his fervent steadiness and inspiration. He held nothing back, offering his unbridled expression of insight and awakening honed by long years of both intensive Vipassana meditation practice and psychotherapy. He taught the simplicity of Buddhist meditation suffused with the fragrance of plumeria and night-blooming jasmine, accompanied by the sweetness of the Sufi poems and his own, all singing his great love affair with the Beloved.

Thanks to the disciplined attention he gave to every aspect of his health and survival, Gavin felt well enough to take the huge risk of moving away from his doctors and the life he cherished in Hawai'i. Without fanfare, he went to live in Mt. Shasta near his beloved teacher Devaji. There he was given the name Saucha, translated as purity of heart. Indeed, Saucha threw himself into the life in Mt. Shasta with pure devotion. Living in the company of Devaji's students, illumined by his vivid awareness of mortality and impermanence, he was purely present. He never missed a retreat or satsang.

With Devaji, Saucha found what he'd been looking for all his life. The healing power of Devaji's fearless love transformed the dregs of childhood sexual and physical abuse into infinite grace and blessing. And Saucha was ready. I'd watched him grow like a mountain through the years of our Big Island visits, simplifying his life more and more, living in inner solitude and joy. I love remembering the sound of Saucha's laughter. His playful high spirits were contagious and could light up the room. The strength of Saucha's intuition, trust, and resolve brought him closer and closer to Devaji and to his many friends in their tight-knit community.

Saucha delighted in the mountain with its two volcanic peaks, Shasta and Shastina. Two peaks, one Mt. Shasta: a majestic symbol of the two-fold practice erupting from the depths of molten love at the center of Saucha's life and ours. I miss my cherished friend. I can hear him calling to us all—Look! Can you catch a glimpse of the immensity of this boundless love? One mountain, one life, one love—only appearing to be divided in two, as self and other. Understanding this comforts me. I stay connected to a being I deeply love. We humans meet, connect, go apart, and meet again in the whirlwind of life and death. In reality, there's no separation, just the twirling dance of falling in love with our self, with each other, and the whole topsy-turvy world.

Only One Surrender is a book of beauty. Rashani took on the mysterious task of translating and decanting the essence of Saucha's poetry into sacred art. An alchemist of imagery, Rashani transmutes his eloquent words for the wordless into sublime visual compositions—sometimes whimsical, sometimes profound, always radiant. They are luminous mandalas of aloha, peace and harmony.

A mountain of mahalo* to you, Rashani, for loving these poems into a new incarnation. *Only One Surrender* is a brilliant tribute to Gavin Saucha Harrison, full of grace. Gavin died a happy man, spiritually fulfilled.

*Mahalo = Hawaiian for thank you

Trudy Goodman,
April 4th, 2019

Saucha's September/October Newsletter, 2018

Beloved Companions, It is the nature of the mind to want to feel safe; to know what is going to happen in an imagined future. Yet we are living in the time when external certainty, security and predictability is increasingly revealing itself to be the illusion it always has been. Whether it's a hurricane, the activity of Goddess Pele, the desecration of the environment, the political climate, the economy, violence or all the flavors of bigotry and unkindness—perhaps the worldly play has never felt so universally unstable and unpredictable.

However, if there is a willingness to not follow the movements and interpretations of mind and instead rest deeply in the present, in the Now, there is an increasing recognition of an inherent and unchanging safety, peace, joy and freedom that has nothing to do with what's going on around us. This is our True Nature. This is who we really are. When there is no projection into the dream of a future, one begins to realize that the external play of change, which once dictated our degree of happiness or unhappiness, is increasingly irrelevant. We stabilize in the light and luminosity of our being, which does not come and does not go. This is true freedom. This is unconditional love. And then there is the possibility of moving out into the world from the unfathomable wisdom of our hearts, instruments of love and peace; in the world but not of the play of the world

Every retreat, every talk, every meditation and every Spiritual Direction/Mentoring session singularly points to this sacred possibility and realization. This is the birthright of all of us.

Saucha's October/November Newsletter, 2018

Beloved Companions, I am excited and immeasurably grateful to be coming home
to the beloved Big Island on Wednesday this week.

There is a silent loveliness within all of us that has absolutely nothing to do with the presence or absence of noise. This ground of peace and beauty is who we are; immaculate because it has never been touched by circumstance; eternal because it's who we have always been and always will be. In community and togetherness, this retreat is an opportunity to turn towards the unspeakable beauty of our true and silent nature; to leave the hustle and bustle of everyday life behind, and remember the glory of who we really are; forgotten perhaps, yet always awaiting our arrival!

October 5th, 2018:

In three weeks, on Wednesday, October 24, 2018, I will be back home on the sacred Big Island, I am excited and immeasurably grateful. To be in communion and togetherness with Sangha and Family is such great blessing. To surrender once again into our companionship of silence, satsang and retreat is grace beyond measure —another opportunity, to turn together towards the Beloved Truth of who we really are, our shared devotion to and Celebration of Truth, Love and this holy moment.

Describing the Indescribable is a divine madness and impossibility. Perhaps for you too, words like God, Unconditional Love, the Peace that passes all Understanding, Allah, Nirvana, Yahweh, the Absolute all carry a fragrance, nectar and vibration of unity, freedom and a love so unfathomably beautiful. Perhaps the mind is humbled into silence.... and with grace we find ourselves steeped in the Holy and Sacred mystery of the Indescribable — a remembrance and recognition of our True Nature and the very truth of existence itself, of reality. This I call "The Beloved." And every poem is a humble homage to the Beloved.

A quote from his website:

We awaken to the sacred ground of Love, Awareness and Joy that was always there, perhaps unrecognized, yet abiding and full beyond description. This Truth of our Being reveals itself as Simple Silence, Infinite Wisdom and Boundless Compassion. The teachings and poetry of Awakening are invitations into the Truth of our Being. By neither bypassing nor transcending our humanness, but embracing it fully, the Love we are flowers and extends across the immensity of time and space touching the greatest and smallest of things.

Gavin was on his way to Hawai'i when he died and I was on my way to greet him at the airport when I got the call that he was not coming. The shock. The indescribable sadness. And then the grace and celebration of his liberation from his Miraculous body that he no longer had need for.

> My beloved sweet Saucha
> You dove perfectly
> Into the ocean of pure consciousness.
> Out of the surf came the wisdom of our hearts
> And in a wet embrace we are one
> In peace, unconditional love and joy,
> In the freedom of our True Nature
> The infinite emptiness of bliss.

So ironic that it was in his boundlessly loving heart his passing occurred. As his doctor, I can attest that at the time, Saucha was never healthier, and had no cardiovascular risk factors except that he owed his life to decades of antiretroviral therapy, that can increase the risk of myocardial Infarction.

Over these same decades, I have been honored to know Rashani, and it is such a blessing she is gracing us with this testament to Saucha through her wonderful collages and his loving words. Om Namah Shivaya,

–**Michael Traub**, Kona, Hawai'i

Gavin Harrison was a force of nature. He lived ten lifetimes on three continents in his almost 70 years. He faced obstacles from boyhood onward, each of which propelled him more deeply into his spiritual journey. In that he was unstoppable. He danced with death all those years and decades, and death waited until after he had transformed into Saucha. At his new home in Mt Shasta, Gavin-become-Saucha had even more deep realizations in the presence of a newly beloved teacher and community.

My husband Jim and I knew Gavin from the time of his diagnosis when he was practicing at IMS, so we journeyed half a life together. In each stage of his geographic transition, he found a home with us, and with it, a circle of caregivers. The last time we saw Gavin, he poured out his passion and his poetry to this circle. We felt like Hafez had entered the space through Gavin. The room could barely contain his enormous devotion and ardor.

Not long afterwards, Gavin's heart gave out in mid-air, his spirit soaring onward.

–**Paula Green**, Leverett Massachusetts

I go to sleep missing and loving my dear friend Saucha Gavin Harrison who died unexpectedly last night. I have been with him on the precipice of death many times before over the past 30 years. But last night he had a heart attack in an airport while on his way to serve others. Though I must find another term because Gavin's heart would never attack anyone let alone his own sweet soul.

Born in South Africa, honored by H.H the Dalai Lama, he lived many lifetimes in this one precious life. Monk, poet, sweet loyal friend, meditator, author, protector of sea turtles, activist, spiritual teacher and lover of the Divine. A life fully lived. Kind heart, tenacious body, boundless mind, beloved spirit I trust you know the way. Walk awe inspired in the radiance of the Mystery.

–**Frank Ostaseski**, Sausalito, California

A few lines from his poem found in *Petals and Blood*, his collection of love poems to *Ecstasy, Awakening, and Annihilation*:

The Bridge to Nowhere

Don't be too quick
to cross the threshold
from this world
to the one calling you Home.

You may wish to hesitate
for a moment
before beginning
your Great Adventure.

For the bridge upon which you walk
shall disappear behind you.

And a great unknowingness
will obscure the way ahead.

Listen to the voices of madness
calling you Home.

Come naked into The Mystery.

Toss your garments to the winds.

This is a high path, no railings.

Everything for nothing.

Welcome to the insane asylum.

If deep within you
there lives a devotion to this insanity,
keep walking.

If not, hug tight your clothing.

Return to the land of the sleeping.

You may wish to move swiftly.

Remember,
the bridge is disappearing
behind you.

Oops!

You have probably
crossed the line already.

Here,
hold my hand.

It takes one lunatic
to recognize another.

It has been a number of years since I've been with Gavin. At a distance of half a globe, there was only an impression —that he continued to spread his wings ever wider and soar ever higher, while as surely present firmly on Gaia.

We think of Gavin with his immense delight, his passion and glowing engagement. We think of Gavin with his excitement, warmth and reaching out. All that is so. I also think of Gavin sharing with me his beloved South Africa— giraffes and zebras wandering through the guest cottages at a Kwazulu preserve; being with him and his mother at their home near Durban; sitting at the Buddhist Retreat Center at Ixopo.

I think of Gavin in respect to his incredible discipline facing the most extreme challenge. Discipline being truly knowing what you love and trust and staying with it, no matter the challenge. And he did. Diet certainly helped. Exercise helped. But it seems certain that practice was the extraordinary life giver. He journeyed multiple times into the raging fires and came through. It is fair to so call body temperatures of 105+. That was being present.

Based in the practice he was able to stay with the pain, the challenges, that defeat most. He remained unconquered and able to share his passion and joy well more than 30 years longer than expected.

—**Rand Engel**, Newburyport, Massachusetts

INTRODUCTION

I had the great joy of meeting Saucha—then known as Gavin—in the 1990's, shortly after he arrived on the Big Island of Hawai'i. We shared an immediate affinity—being fervent lovers of nature and poetry, deeply-rooted in the Mystery, devoted to finding the miraculous in the ordinary; reveling in the seamlessness of the absolute and the relative. Emptiness and form. Having both lived in Europe and on Turtle Island, and having both been summoned to this volcanic paradise of paradox in the middle of the Pacific Ocean, we bowed—together and alone—in reverence and gratitude to the ancestral presence and to the untamableness of this island, to its rugged and delicate beauty, diversity and fecundity, and to the "aloha spirit," which is a fundamental aspect of the Hawaiian culture.

We were both deeply influenced by indigenous people—cross culturally; by their primordial grace, sovereignty, simplicity, depth, and wisdom. We were both dedicated activists and allies to marginalized beings and used our gifts to raise money for those in need. And, we both devoted our lives to sharing with others—through nature, art and poetry—the "living (ungraspable) dharma," and were not afraid to address the issues of homophobia, sexism and racism within the Buddhist community.

In the Vipassana tradition the teacher is seen as a spiritual guide or friend, unlike other Buddhist traditions. Saucha was "uniequal." *Unique and equal* to/with everyone. He was an accessible friend for many; an evocator of grace, a wise mentor—a maverick of sorts—who continued to cross his own edges as they arose. His humanness and ferocious self-accountability and his willingness and capacity to cultivate open attention allowed him to constantly evolve—and kept him authentically connected with his students, colleagues and friends; with all of life.

A true servant of the Heart—unwaveringly committed to love—Saucha was intimately acquainted with the complexities of the human psyche, the pitfalls and ego traps of the landless path, the seductive nature of spiritual bypassing, and the subtle intricacies of the soul-domain of essence—and emptiness. Sunyata.

Having witnessed apartheid in South Africa and having been given many opportunities to transform opposition into opportunity, he was tumbled & humbled, hollowed and hallowed by life—transformed by grace again and again—and became an accomplished alchemist and a radiant beacon of love; a luminous wisdom lamp for many. He was a grounded mystic who rested in a chasm of fire *and* in the lap of the Buddha, while simultaneously being fully immersed in the agony and ecstasy, the horror and the beauty; the wretchedness and gloriousness of this earth walk called life.

When Death Comes by Mary Oliver:

When death comes
like the hungry bear in autumn;
when death comes and takes all the bright coins from
his purse
to buy me and snaps the purse shut;
when death comes
like the measle-pox;
when death comes
like an iceberg between the shoulder blades,
I want to step through the door full of curiosity,
wondering
what is it going to be like, that cottage of darkness?
And therefore, I look upon everything
as a brotherhood and a sisterhood,
and I look upon time as no more than an idea,
and I consider eternity as another possibility,

and I think of each life as a flower, as common
as a field daisy, and as singular,
and each name a comfortable music in the mouth,
tending, as all music does, toward silence,
and each body a lion of courage, and something
precious to the earth.
When it's over, I want to say all my life
I was a bride married to amazement,
I was the bridegroom, taking the world into my arms.
When it's over, I don't want to wonder
if I have made of my life something particular, and
real.
I don't want to find myself sighing and frightened
or full of argument.
I don't want to end up simply having visited this
world.

I imagine Saucha "stepping through the door full of curiosity" and he certainly was more than simply a visitor here on planet Earth. He tenderly, and sometimes fiercely—and always whole-heartedly—took the world into his arms.

Saucha's memorial service, two months ago, was indescribable. Loved ones and members of his sangha gathered on a beautiful afternoon at Hapuna beach, west of Kona. Manyness and Oneness simultaneously celebrating the life of this deeply-loved, one of a kind, radiant being. The circle was suffused with emptiness and fullness, grief and gratitude, celebration and tears, absence and presence. Though Saucha was physically absent he was as present as the afternoon light interacting with the waves and white sand; as joyous as the laughter of children playing on the beach, as sweet as the sublime fragrance of gardenia and plumeria blossoms. His boundless spirit felt at times like a huge lei—and other times like the golden wings of Garuda—or a phoenix—tenderly holding the entire circle.

On the way home I passed Kealakekua, Hoʻokena, and Miloliʻi where there are several enormous Jacaranda trees. I knew that in less than six months their branches would be clustered with brilliant lavender/blue-violet flames. In Kealakekua, there are also several magnificent Prima Vera trees—with the brightest yellow blossoms I have ever seen. Brighter than goldenrod or daffodils, sunflowers or pansies. For nearly thirty years, between late winter and early spring, these two colors have stunned my eyes every time I saw them. Occasionally I thought to myself, "One day I will design a collage with these amazing colors."

Here it is—the center of the cover of this small tribute to Saucha Gavin. And these colors continue echoing through the book. You will also see Islamic calligraphy and other symbols interwoven into these pages—to celebrate the diversity of the expression of timeless wisdom and to pay homage to Saucha's love for the Middle East. The Persian calligraphy on the dedication page is the word, "heech," which means *no-thing*. The calligraphy at the bottom of this page is "Alhamdulillah," which means *praise be to God*—or *thank God*. The title and subtitle are both excerpts from two different poems by Saucha, which called out to me.

I have felt Saucha's presence more than usual while piecing this book together. Thank you, Matilda Tompson, for giving me permission to share excerpts of his poems in this way. Most of them are from his book, *Petals and Blood: Stories, Dharma & Poems of Ecstasy, Awakening & Annihilation,* and a few are from poems that Saucha read aloud and shared on his website.

Saucha often remained calm in the face of difficult challenges and offered to others—both directly with words, and indirectly, by example—a simple, uncontrived, compassionate, and often contagious way of being. He was a great catalyst and "spiritual Sherpa" of sorts—for those who were ready to relinquish their false identities and deconstruct the unquestioned beliefs, which prevented their full awakening. It feels appropriate to end here with this Hawaiian proverb, which refers to a person who can remain centered and calm in the face of difficulty:

He poʻi na kai uli, kai koʻo, ʻaʻohe hina pukoʻa.
Though the sea be deep and rough, the coral rock remains standing.

Love pours forth~

Rashani Rea,
Imbolc, 2019

What is your heart's deepest longing?

What is most important in your life right now?

Be available to the grace and the good fortune already upon its way
and bow before the sacred possibilities
of this time together.

"Allah is eternal"

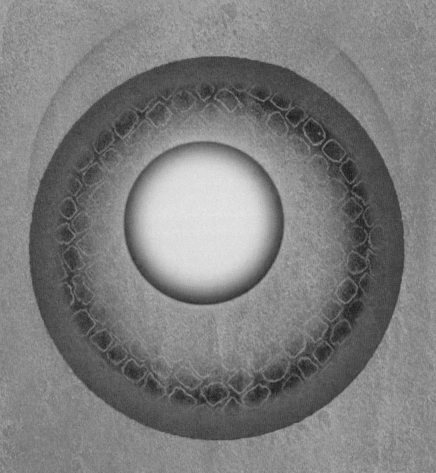

In the end there is only one surrender.
Everything.
Nowhere to go. You are already there.

"Mu"

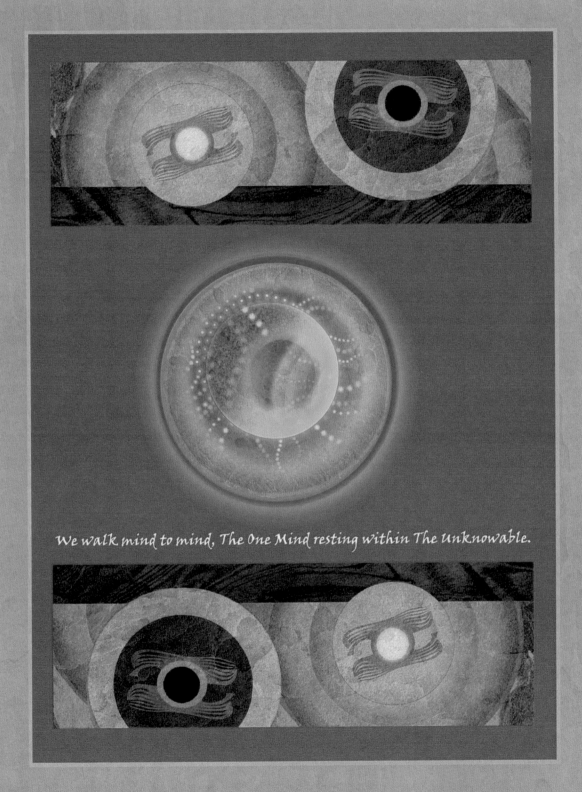

We walk mind to mind, The One Mind resting within The Unknowable.

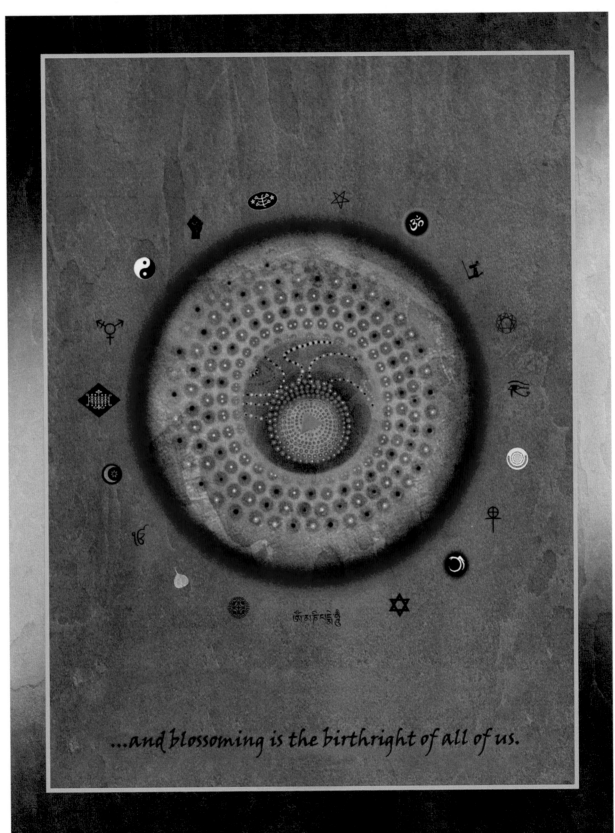

...and blossoming is the birthright of all of us.

Please kneel beside me as I bow before the forgetfulness of a lifetime
and turn back towards the one I left behind.

"Freedom"

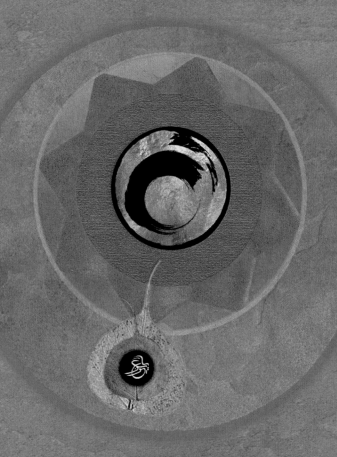

Occupy your indignation
that anything less than liberation will just not do.

"The unconquerable"

May your heart release its gift before thought and self-involvement obscure the limiting possibilities   ahead of you.

عشق

"Love"

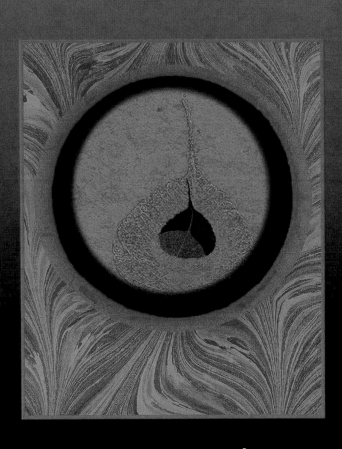

It is just as well I did not know how unforgiving Your demand for self-honesty would be. For the fire of that injunction would have been way too hot for me to handle.

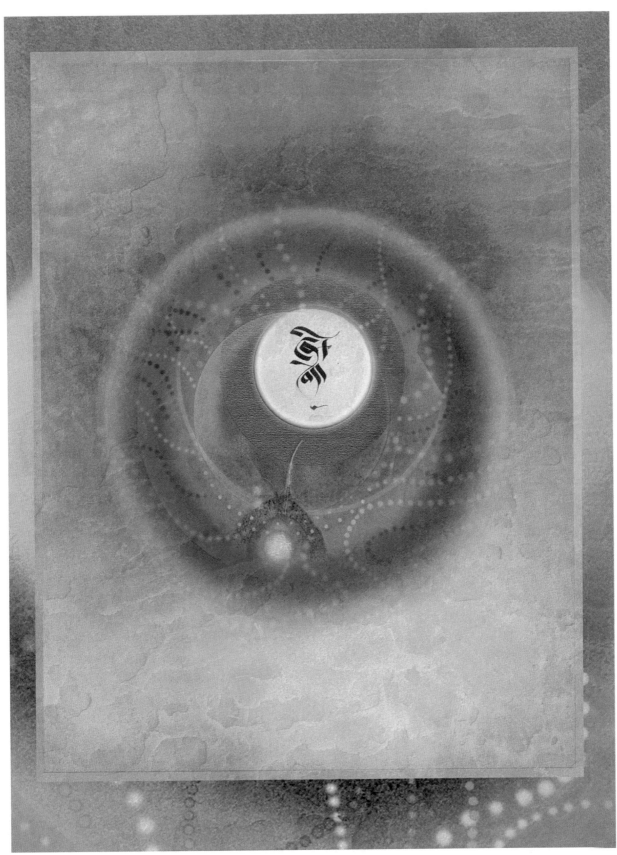

"Impermanence"

It is just as well I did not know how many lines You would have me cross. For I would have gripped my prison bars more tightly in terror than ever before.

we are NOT ALONe

we are NOT ALONe.
LOVers OF MYSTerY and adVeNTUre
HaVe already eNTered THe POrTaLS OF OUr TOGeTHerNeSS.

Be dazzled by the realm of reflection
and refraction.

...you shall come upon your True Nature, not by design nor will,
but by happenstance and grace.

Give way into the sacred arc of your life.

"In the name of Allah, most gracious, most merciful"

It is just as well I did not know how simple and ordinary this that I Am would turn out to be.

For the specialness and grandiosity that once lived here would have had nothing

to do with the Quietude and Emptiness that is here now.

"All returns to emptiness"

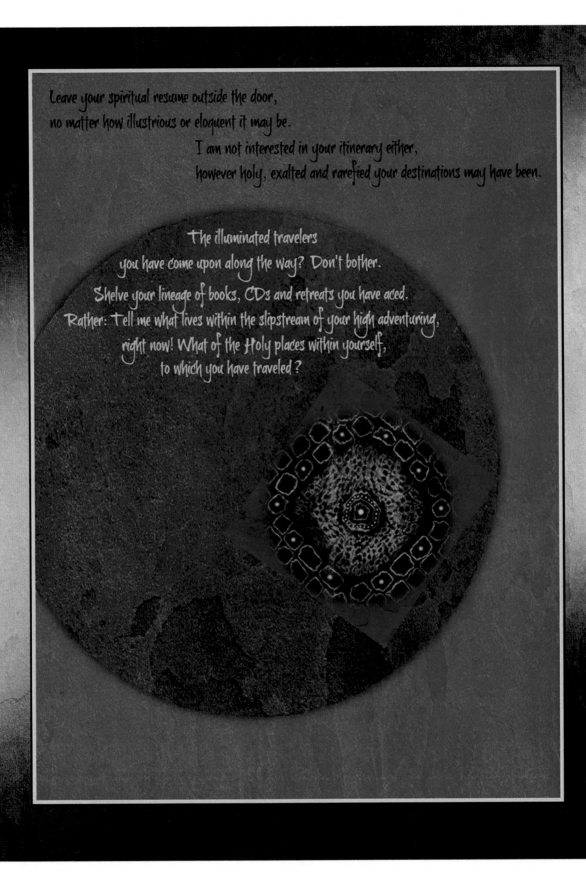

Leave your spiritual resume outside the door,
no matter how illustrious or eloquent it may be.

I am not interested in your itinerary either,
however holy, exalted and rarefied your destinations may have been.

The illuminated travelers
you have come upon along the way? Don't bother.

Shelve your lineage of books, CDs and retreats you have aced.
Rather: Tell me what lives within the slipstream of your high adventuring,
right now! What of the Holy places within yourself,
to which you have traveled?

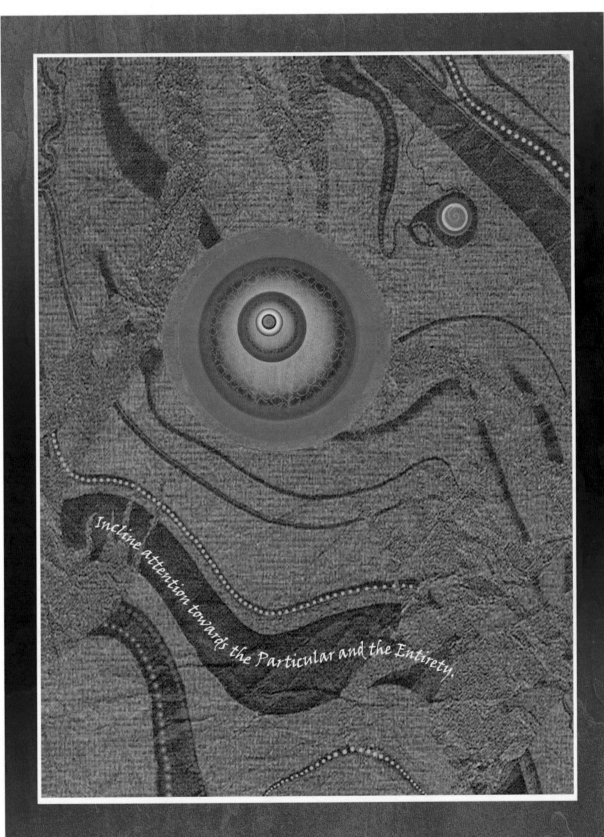

Incline attention towards the Particular and the Entirety.

We walk heart to heart
in whatever direction the unfolding of love moves us.

"Life is good"

GIVE YOURSELF TO THE INTERMINGLING OF GREAT HEARTS LONGING FOR HOME.

*Raise your fist. Open. Grab the sky. Touch
the ground. Seize your birthright. Unfurl great
wings. Occupy all streets everywhere with your loving.*

七転八起

"Fall down 7 times, get up 8"

In the end there is only one love. It does not come, it does not go.

This love is who you are. Abiding and beyond describing.
Why settle for less?

Resist not the difficult person
standing before you right now.

This one is a Divine Emissary
pointing towards that within you,
ready to join
The Great Story of your life.

Feel your connection with this one.

It is there, like it or not.

Be not against
what is given you.

Whatever is rejected
obscures the glory
of who you truly are.

Give
what you want the most from others.

Hear the Hounds of Heaven
yapping at your ankles.

The Assembly of Angels
is already singing
your song of Homecoming.

Don't procrastinate a moment longer.

Stop the war.

Welcome
the wild winds of circumstance
and the challenges before you,
Emissaries all
from Our Beloved,
calling you Home
without delay.

Disdain
the subterfuge
of separation and resistance,
however eloquent
the dexterity of your justification
might be.

Keep your eyes on The Prize
of
this precious, precious life.

Fortify what you are for,
not against.

For
Our Beloved
will continue to provide you
with Emissaries
until it is no longer necessary
to do so.

COME NAKED INTO THE MYSTERY.

"Alhamdulillah"

Other books by Saucha Gavin Harrison include:

IN THE LAP OF THE BUDDHA

PETALS AND BLOOD: Stories, Dharma & Poems of Ecstasy, Awakening & Annihilation

Other books by Rashani Réa include:

BEYOND BROKENNESS. The Danish version is called "SANGEN I SORGEN"

THE TIME OF TRANSFORMATION IS HERE

CHAKRA POEMS

A SOFT IMMINENCE OF RAIN: Celtic Poems by Alice O. Howell

A CRY OF WINDBELLS

MY BIRD HAS COME HOME

THE UNFURLING OF AN ARTIST: Early Collages and Calligraphy of Rashani Réa

WELCOME TO THE FEAST: In Celebration of Wholeness

IS THE BOWL EMPTY OR IS IT FILLED WITH MOONLIGHT: Turning Words and Bodhi Leaves

THE WAY MOONLIGHT TOUCHES

MAHALO: Visual Koans for the Pathless Journey

ALWAYS CHOOSE LOVE

MOONLIGHT ON A NIGHT MOTH'S WING: A Fusion of Image and Word

TRUE GOLDEN SAND

TIMELESS OFFERINGS

SHIMMERING BIRTHLESS: A Confluence of Verse and Image

AN UNFOLDING OF LOVE

TOUCHED BY GRACE: Through a Temenos of Women

TERRITORY OF WONDER

GOSSAMER MIRRORS

IN PRAISE OF LOVE: A Dialogue Between a Dove and a Ladybug

THE DISAPPEARANCE

THE THRESHOLD BETWEEN LOSS AND REVELATION co-authored with Francis Weller

A BRIEF COLLISION WITH CLOCKOCRACY

I CAN HEAR HER BREATHING

COLLABORATING WITH THE INEVITABLE

THE FIRE OF DARKNESS: What Burned Me Away Completely, I Became

THREE CHILDREN'S STORIES, which include: *PRESENT MOMENT, COLORFUL MOMENT: Sharing Present Moment Awareness with Children, TAO AND THE MOON, and CAN YOU DRAW A SHOOTING STAR?: A Child's Experience and Expression of Loss.*

Rashani also created collections of collages for *LEAVES FROM MOON MOUNTAIN* by Dorothy Hunt and *GATHERING SILENCE* by Ivan M. Granger.

Saucha had a lifelong commitment to support orphaned and vulnerable children and those who care for them at The Woza Moya Project and The Group of Hope in South Africa. The Woza Moya Project runs a community-care and support program in the Ofafa Valley, near the town of Ixopo in KwaZulu-Natal, South Africa. Partial proceeds from the sale of this book will be sent to the Woza Moya Project and The Group of Hope.